Fusion

Matt Duggan
Jennie E Owen
Briony Collins
Si Griffiths
Wendy Sinnamon
Adam Panichi

Edited by Alan Parry

Fusion Poets: One
Edited by Alan Parry

Brought to you by The Broken Spine

Art and Literature

ISBN: 9798335637817

© Alan Parry, 2024. All rights reserved.

Book design: Alan Parry and Andrew James Lloyd
Cover Image: MidJourney
Cover Composition: Andrew James Lloyd
Edited by Alan Parry
All copyright to individual texts are held and reserved by the authors

The Broken Spine Ltd
Southport / England / United Kingdom
www.thebrokenspine.co.uk

'Success is best when it's shared.'

Howard Schultz

Fusion Poets: One

Matt Duggan
Jennie E. Owen
Briony Collins
Si Griffiths
Wendy Sinnamon
Adam Panichi

Edited by Alan Parry

Contents

1	*Debone & Fold*
	Si Griffiths
3	*Michelin*
4	*Hors D'oeuvres*
5	*Cry Me a Liver*
6	*Enchilada*
7	*Temper Temper*
9	*Chronicle*
	Matt Duggan
11	*A Child's Playground*
12	*Beyond the Green Tower*
14	*Betamax*
15	*Masculinity*
16	*Growing Pains*
17	*Tips for the Collector of the Macabre*
	Jennie E. Owen
19	*Today My Heart Is*
20	*Gran's Axe*
21	*Painting the Dead*
22	*Internment*
24	*Still Life*

25 *I Know Where the Pelicans Go*
    Briony Collins

27 *Pelican Man*
28 *You Could Be Good*
29 *The Last Room*
30 *Going*
31 *I Know Where the Pelicans Go*

33 *Cupid, Grown*
    Adam Panichi

35 *The Boys are Killing Their Sims on the Family PC*
36 *Lilac Bushes*
37 *God in a Bathhouse*
39 *Kleptomania*
40 *After a Mild Electric Shock I Think of England*

41 *The Devouring*
    Wendy Sinnamon

43 *Vitrine*
44 *Drupelet (in three parts)*
47 *Fractals*
48 *Forgiveness*
50 *Outdoor Type*

51 *Acknowledgements*
52 *Recommended Reading*
53 *Author Biographies*

Debone & Fold

Si Griffiths

Michelin

Who's innovation, pressure of perfection, lauded as heroic?
No slip is excused as we ascend this ladder of stars.

*

Who rides the wave that thumps litter strewn shores?
Redundancy inbuilt, detritus disposable, leisure on demand.

*

Who's inspiration, the guide for a worthy detour?
To think that tyre sales would inflate as we deviate.

*

Hors D'oeuvres

It must take an hour for us to order,
the waitress keeps coming back,
first with a smile, later a laugh.
And seriously, we do try to spend
just a minute with that menu.

But here we sit, hand-locked, eyes held.
Not one kiss has passed this table's lips,
across its white linen I tease,
my drum-roll feathered, a play,
palm to forearm.

Our talk a fusilli of twists and turns,
vegan ice cream to theories of change.
Your words alert against mine,
a rehearsal of a sort, an embrace
of a kind.

Finally, we decide, then pick and push around our plates.

A first date, an online match,
but what code could predict this mix?
Set a whisk to work, the friction of heat
and air leaving us both almost
fit to explode.

I look up and am struck, tables cleared,
chairs on end, a thicket of dark wooden spikes.
We ease ourselves out, all giggles and thanks,
gentle, as between us there's egg white
ready to fold.

Cry Me a Liver

All around our house, hundreds of lambs;
floppy on just found hooves, gangs
of curious huddles that push and cajole.

Nothing like summer's athletic teens,
or the night they're taken with dogs and quads,
the whole hillside a siren of howls and screams.

The insistent bawl of these valleys,
thousands of mothers, each with her call.
Where are you? Come back to me.

The farmer, stoic, says the first night's the worst,
but they continue, into the second and third,
as if sensing a treadmill, six weeks, pregnant again.

Or maybe it's the fate of their young, that journey:
abattoir, butcher's block, red chopping board,
trimmed down to a liver, its texture

a rich purple sponge. Sliced and sizzled
in a deep, dark rue, served with one bacon
streak on a cake of bubble and squeak.

Enchilada

I bring your salad to my lips, the clean, crisp cut of lime.
Guacamole with it's cream, your stone, my fruit,
the tender test of touch. Firm to start, but as we warm,
so you soften. The rich depths of your sauce,
my tongue, your taste, salt and dark.
Black beans refried, the salsa green,
layer the contrasts, let them build, our edges
wrapped by the bliss of this flour lipped kiss.
Flatbread hot pan flipped, it's double 'L' a 'Y',
when I use my teeth.

Tôr-tē′yə.

Temper Temper

A
day
is all
I need
to bring
you down,
without me
who are you.
I hold the key.
All this is mine,
gateway to slice
this veil and halve
the world, my edge
hard, my will unbent
never yielding. I hoard
and huddle over knicks
let them fester on blade
battle scarred, my forge
burns, yet always ready
I chip, chop,
slice, dice.
I cut, gut,
fillet and
fuck you
up. Such
poise and
so deft. Do
not deviate, no
kink or knot can
disarm this steel,
hard, tempered,
my hilt, jewel
strewn with
all these
skulls.

Chronicle

Matt Duggan

Beyond the Green Tower

Beyond green towers beside town houses
two flights of stairs –we dropped flowers,
from high-rises, that fell like drowning,
paper ships- pirouetting between
shut windows where children's
broken toys would sit.
my brother, hooligan of terraces,
idolised Wham until George came out of the cold –
he wore his warrior gene to football games,
like must a bigger man took aim.
Together we watched swallows,
spin from flats, heard traffic,
rise above towers, painted,
in luminous orb green & yellow.
where I saw my best friend sectioned,
for wearing Nike sneakers,
on top of his head – convinced,
he was invisible to everyone -
after eating peyote – shop assistant
mildly amused at this young boy
high   on vivid hallucinogens.

A Child's Playground

My father sold carpets,
not magical enough to fly away,
or to buy us all a Berni Steak –

we spent summer, in mimetic,
realms of green levelled forests,
made of chocolate coloured snuff
valley of silver washed slate,

Robin Hood & Oliver Cromwell
wandered barren lands to the local estate,
these grounds held my palms,
like deserts to a man dying of thirst.

It's where I first drowned as a boy,
leg hooked in by short reeds,
like tight knots of fishing nets
dragging me under water

until a god like man's hand reached down,
pulled me to the surface,
we played out war, with oak revolvers-
sometimes as stormtroopers,

among lavender thistle,
brown laces of fallen fern tree,
now and then we played as Jedi,
our lightsabers long twigs,

painted a luminous bright yellow,
we swerved pages of naked women,
camouflaged in long grass,

among darts of pollen
hidden by a centrefold in Razzle.

Betamax

Evidenced our existence on black reels   & Star Wars figures,
we roll creased Betamax ribbon   with a blue biro pen,
we spent last year   unravelling   boxes of bones,
decades full of whitened   slurs   tried capturing,
what was left behind   thought we were the coolest of kids –
first   in the neighbourhood   watch video films
until we discovered   everyone else in the street   had VHS.

Masculinity

Why must men　　　　　　　never be fragile?
Figures determined　　　　stanchion of strength,
it is much harder to see　　　　damaged goods,
when guarding　　　　every panoply of armour
when shapes of a fist –　　　　continue rule,
who taught you　　(Who taught you how to fight?)
we understand　　　　frailty/ delicacy/ fragility,
among the young　　rarely do we think of timidity.

Growing Pains

Always the same stereotypical conjecture
when did it happen, when did you learn to curve,
like a serpent limbs switch sides - did you pucker up lips –
stand on two feet, did you take the first hit,
did you cry, when taking, a full-grown man's hand?
do you remember, first time not the time,
you ejaculated into a sock, not fumbling,
embarrassment to losing one's virginity,
time you made a stand to fight,
remember first beating,
collapsed in a ditch at midnight,
concerned more, about claret, on a bloodied,
Garfield T-shirt   than flatness to a bloodied broken nose.
Dad be proud of you, if you knocked   a man out cold,
you return home - lump knuckles   fractured eye-socket,
nostrils tasted like sulphur   never wore Ben Sherman
rain fed sun on a day - you were born of apples-
limp in night   visions of passing cars, along   asphalt
between two bridges   glue-sniffers   slept on tarpaulin,
pretending to be portions of yellow light.

Tips for the Collector of the Macabre

Jennie E. Owen

Today my heart is

Lighter nights, the bird song after a long winter.
A shallow grave in the rain on the side of a mountain.

The salty sounds and smells of the fairground; the swaying, the lights!
A clown slipping on a banana skin into the mouth of a waiting tiger.

The feeling when you plunge your bare hand deep into the snow,
followed by the burn on your face when you come back inside

Yours, yours and always yours,
but never mine (not even the tip of the left ventricle)

All the scandalous and exciting things I hope they might be saying.
The reality that they didn't even see me there.

Diving into the Mediterranean Sea from a dusty dockside,
knowing there might be sharks shadowing beneath the surface.

The feeling of safety when I can see you don't know.
The look on your face the day you found out.

That soft undulating tone you used to say my name.
Our favourite child's coffin.

The swirl of starlings, ink in a water sky.
Two magpies fighting over the corpse of next doors puppy by moonlight (is that a wolf howl I hear?)

In your hands dearest reader, I dare you to give it a squeeze.

Gran's Axe

As she told it,
my grandmother watched,
salt pillared
the street. Whilst a man
swung at
 a child, to cleave
the head in two,
to yawn it red open.

The story became,
and so, turned to the footnote
of her tragedy.

All the players
now lie stiff as tin soldiers, they await
unwritten scenes.

My grandmother's own baby,
was first born
blue from the shock.

The memories themselves,
in turn are now lost, only
the words trickle down,
mouth to mouth.

They scream spit
into the faces of ghosts.

Painting the Dead

Room lighting is key for the task
bright daylight, the best. Old newspapers
essential to catch the spills, plus kitchen paper
to suction excess drops. I recommend
mixing the colours in an old dish, the lid
of a margarine tub. A jam jar.

I started of course, with hand tinting photos,
bringing back the glow of black and white
brides, children at the beach,
the pink in the lips of memento mori.
The flesh tones are the hardest, they require
a lightness of touch, a deftness God given.
I blow life and pigments, gentle exhalations
tremble across the surface.

There is no longer a need to advertise my craft.
They come to me, knock at my door. I find
tiny coffins, or gifts of feathers and leaves
that wash up and spill cross my floor.
Two or three times a day: a limb, an ear,
a lifted brow to piece together.

You cannot bring back the dead I warn them
as I warm the lips and chaff the skin,
but you can colour and frame them,
hang them brightly in the next room.

Internment

This is a time of death you tell yourself,
brushing back your hair, polishing buttons

all lined up in a row. This is the work of death
and you have carried friends, family – this is no different

if you do not think of their faces
how the fire burned the clothes off their very bodies.

You pull at your jacket, remind yourself
that this is a time of death. That God is greedy,

the papers record a daily exodus from life
across the globe. Many, will not return to their

villages and towns, some will simply vanish.
This is an honour, you tell yourself, to carry a child

in a time of death, in a coffin so light
that it only takes only two fighting men

to carry, to walk the procession like hard
backed beetles with identical corsages. Through

the streets with their guard of honour, their families
six bodies deep. So few children among them.

Yet too many little coffins to fit into the church,
they will lie outside, side by side

all lined up in a row. After
you will pass the coffin to the red face man

stood low in the grave, then your job will be done.
You will try not to avoid the gaze of the mothers

They understand that this is a grey sky time of death
when lives exist briefly to be lost or won.

Still Life

a wild bloom in the bent arm of the brook,
mossy infant all pink eared balsam,
pale stemmed. Rooted, naked and tangle-jointed,
under the low sky. Skin a mother's lips
could have warmed now cool as the water,
that moves him, running
where a heart should have beaten
its moths wings.

He awaits discovery, wet muzzles
to worry over him gently like a bone.

Only a bone.

In sleep, his fingers open blue petals,
a puzzle,
too small,
to hold the world so vast.

I Know Where the Pelicans Go

Briony Collins

Pelican Man

front feathers warble

        jugulate plumage
a beak, agape, rockets
                pitched-down dial-up
        preens engine song
from a shudder start

                            he turns into a man

sheds his quill clusters
        steps forth plucked flesh
follicles raw, dotted
                strawberry seeds
        indented evidence
of nudity

a new cry from open lips
        wheeze like mildew
spore and gasp
                grey lung matter
        bare chest shaking
a human rapture

                            no one sees him change

clacks an absent bill
        fuzzing sparse white hair
between baldness
                this world forgets him
        pouches his weight
and flies away

You Could Be Good

Young boys gathered at the bay:
footballs and sandcastles.
This is where their mums told them they were good
and in those words they found a life to make warm,
to hold in their hands like a newborn, a soft head
cupped in a calloused hand, swooning at the scent
of milk and Sudocrem. They believed it. This is where
they became fathers, at the shoreline of teenagedom,
the future unrolled like a birth, like a wave bursting,
gathering froth and sparkling into calm, where they first
knew they could do it, one day, and do it well.
Then the grey sea coughed against rocks, lurked in pools,
sought them in the moats they carved with spades,
swept away worm castings and brought half-rotten crabs,
reminded them of the way of things.

The Last Room

Light, nictitating membrane,
        sheaths dark under the door

Walls deepen nicotine stares,
        part from the empty bed

Rheumatic fever splits sweat
        He holds himself

Who would stop him now
        from going outside

Going

Sack your class off; don't go to work
Nothing they say means anything real

Don't go in today; it doesn't matter
The going is never what matters

Summer goes – sticky traps catch gnats
Whisper legs syruped in hypnosis
Yellow makes dust of them
Of eggs pressing in their abdomens

And autumn unrolls like a lizard's tongue
At first the tug of a rusted jaw
Then the snap and stick of muscle spurt
Jellying insects deep

The pelicans go – nurse migratory patterns
Duck southern wind ducts for months
Billowing fish and feather stench
Digest their caviar blues

Summer goes – it curls around itself
Like a class like a job like a tongue like a dying thing
Like an anchovy squeeze gullet sucking silver
Oesophageal clench and twist

You go with it

I Know Where the Pelicans Go

They have a pub on the corner of orange and twist
Breadcrumb themselves up the gum-spot slabs
Meander with juttering necks through walnut doors
Slam a wing on the counter and cry whisky
They come for the herringbone floor
Which reminds them of something

They're here every night of the week
And one, with a quid dispersing sweat metal
Rampages up the juke box and kicks a juggle thwarp
Up white throats, the machine eating coins
Like stolen rings, coughs up rough electric
Begins again

His wife at home twitches twigs and eggs
The hatchlings, damp pink membranes, squeal
This is what she was told she was made for
And he – skirting skies, falconing to imbibe
Catches the first bell of the next day

Cupid, Grown

Adam Panichi

The Boys are Killing Their Sims on the Family PC
after Andrew McMillan

Legs crossed under their computer desks
like a pole dancer in an ankle hang, sweating
as if the floor has been deleted,
running their hands over their silken midriff
in the character room's mirror, deciding between
the kitten heel and the thigh high boot. *It's okay.*
Out of view the door is locked, the boys
are taking up floristry, selling their creations,
their prickled thumbs, gardens fragrant
with box shrubs and lavender.
There's no gravestone under the oak tree
so there's no ghost to haunt the lot at night.
They've just finished renovating the guest bathroom
—*aren't the tiles to die for?* — have found
the perfect fuchsia paper for the hall.
How gorgeous their home is when no one's in.
The boys are flirting with Don Lothario, *shh
Nina has no idea!* They've bought a heart-shaped bed, invited
their lovers over. The boys cannot wait
to raise a child, are petrified to the point
of stillness, they've moved the cot beside their bed,
the media is terrified the boys will mimic
what they do behind their screen.
No longer wary of fireplaces or pools of water,
when they talk about Bella Goth the boys
are mixing up their pronouns. If the new sofa
doesn't go, they can always pick a new one.
I feel for all our drowning.

Lilac Bushes
I've got a lot of making up to do.
               - William Leslie Arnold

Behind the vinyl shower curtain a lilac bush,
knotted into the tie around your neck a lilac bush,

floating in the cereal a lilac bush, on the cheek you kiss
your son on before work and halfway

through your favourite jazz record where it skips
a lilac bush. At the school recital you've never missed,

at parent-teacher conference, blossoming from the teacher's
mouth a lilac bush. When you make love to your wife

her skin is lilac fragranced, isn't it? Playing ball with your son
on the lawn, the lawn a lilac meadow. In the kitchen

your wife makes dinner, you wonder how she does it
all those lilac bushes on the counter. During

a sermon on the sinfulness of crime, a lilac bush at the
pulpit. When you pass an airport, cop car or penitentiary.

On every remembered anniversary.
As the reed touches your lips to play, lilac's taste.

William, when the detective finally found
you, someone had laid flowers on your grave.

God in a Bathhouse

Take a look at a Michelangelo,
the one with God in a bath,
God letting the water out, or

putting the plug back in,
God in a bathhouse with hot bathmates.
We shared a room once.

Five years ago, when I slept
in your bed with your
husband, kissed him first,

I didn't mean to stay, I promise
as if it would change anything.
All of life is tricking the head cop.

In the centre of the Atlantic,
news reports say men
are boarding lifeboats

before the women and children,
others are taking the propeller's
way out. It has nothing to do

with a starving idea
everything to do with plucking
a single red grape from a bunch

in a supermarket aisle. Language,
to Nietzsche, is a gaoler.
The poet is always pacing a cell.

In the film, she's doing the mambo
on a log, the lead holding her,
her pretending to fall, hips swaying

as she stumbles, he's weeping.
If you dropped both words
on the moon, they'd land together.

God the iceberg, God pacing
his moon-cell, God in a bathhouse
lifted from water.

Kleptomania

No sooner has the plane touched down
than my fingers go itching to my pickings.
My left pocket offers a dish of lard
from which raises rosemary's woody head,
pilfered the day in your mother's yard
you taught me to spread it over crescentine.
I dog-ear a page of your family
album, cast iron tigelle pans
pressed together on a lit stove top
opposite a tableful of sharing hands.
Then from my ear I pull a stave of language –
A tavola si può far arte.
My blunt tongue springs a summer peach:
hollow and singing as a cathedral.

I hold each in turn to the cold sun,
ask them if they are mine to keep

After a Mild Electric Shock I Think of England

I'm no scientist but I've pressed
a D cell's
        nub
to my tongue,

which is to say
I know electricity.

Maybe you're right
I am biassed
The BS1363 plug: opposite of
        foreign
slips right in

correct in your hand,
an unforeseen keepsake, well-balanced
table-knife.

Sometimes as its earth is sliding
home
I keep my index nested
between its pins
                to feel

            buzzless,

      safe as a
      doorknob.

The Devouring

Wendy Sinnamon

Vitrine

The sun spreads like marmalade
across the walls of our house.
And now, for now
we, me and you
are suspended
in bittersweet.

You are still.
You are still but still
a curler has come loose anyway;
a spent bullet on our carpet.
Gunpowder trails gunpowder smells
Sylvia, you were an explosion.
Made basalt out of me.
Sweet ammonite lips
each groove an artefact of us.

A heartbeat descends on our backyard

        palpitates
death's little familiar
kissed by every winter
a ruby breast
a last caress

my precious jewel.
We shall break this bitter light.
We shall redden the sun with our wings.

Drupelet (in three parts)
For S.H

i.
A familiar rumble ambles around my cul-de-sac: The Grocery Man.
Commanding a van so fit for purpose it looks like a child drew it.
He executes a remarkable three point turn and my neighbour, on the opposite side,
stops burning the weeds that threaten his garden and gazes up at the turning tires,
with a first time father's admiration.
The van slows, stops in front of my house and the Grocery man is: Woman.
My neighbour resumes his ritual incineration of anything that threatens his cultivated garden.
It takes him several attempts to reignite the fire at the end of his stick.
The blue flames curl around a premature dandelion; didn't even get a chance to bloom,
snuffed out before the roots could take hold.

Two huge two dimensional blackberries adorn the side of her perfect van.
Drupelets the size of dying suns; purple.
Poetic licence gone mad.

ii.
I eat crustless sandwiches from a cling film plate, then I try on his great-coat.
Borrowed, for a minute. Then it was someone else's turn.
Late August, given heavy rain and sun
For a full week, the blackberries would ripen.
A bruised applause rippling across hedgerows,
that look like they've been dragged through a hedgerow backwards.

My Dad said that that's what he looked like, with that hair of his.
I would say born rather than dragged.
Incubated inside a single twinkling drupelet. Hanging off the edge of
Bellaghy.

Smooth blackberry scabs. I pick at them as he looks at the picture
the teacher had took.
                    -Small girl, big coat-
I could grow, I said.
Not into that, he said;
never into that.

iii.
Late August.
Peeling jam pots are borrowed from the neighbours.
Cupboard dwelling plastic bags are set free.
We plunge into deep space.
Clusters of inverse stars
ripening at the edge of everything
collapse inside our fists.
Black holes pool on the ground
Scratched and cagouled Gallileos.
We defy gravity.
We drop galaxies into our plastic bags.
Time bends around us.
Our own little universe.

Back on Earth, dusk quickens.
We take a shortcut home.
You made it, you said, when you were a young man
with other young men,
who are still young now.
It's overgrown. My feet fall into grasses as long as funerals.
The dark distorts everything.

I mistake birds for bats and you tut like you do,
I mistake trees for waving giants,
I mistake police sirens for banshee wails.
I mistake the tight grip of your hand for impatience.

I mistook death when it came.
For something that just happens
like a three point turn
or the Big Bang.
But, it's something you grow into,
you said.

Fractals
Latin, fractus - "broken."

Dearest,
       This morning rose like insurgency.
Dawn broke against my window.
A warmth gripped in her valiant fists.
Oh happy grenades!
Should I pull the pin?

Dearest,
       This afternoon enchanted like two magpies,
caught in conversation
spied through a thicket
from the window of a train.

Dearest,
       This evening beat with a pomegranate heart.
Gave its love piecemeal.
Ruby bursts that stained everything.

Forgiveness

I am three days in.
For three days these hands have shook,
these hands have beat back ceaselessly against themselves
quivering like a choir-boy's messianic mandible.
So I sever the nerve,
cut feeling out at the root.

I am a chaos.
A lone seagull harvesting debris
with abandon, and an enviable equanimity.
Insanity is doing the same thing over and over and
expecting different results.

I am three days in.
For three days this skin has shrieked
spewed forth thick apocrine sweat
screamed in Pentecostal tongues
'I am filled with the Holy Spirit!' it says
it says.

I am a hummingbird
stuck in a spider web.
Sky shunned.
Tiny wings beating against a grey trap.
Too large to devour.

I am three days in.
For three days I have exorcised this tongue
plucked it from this demon head.
This tongue is the hydra,
two more will spring from the bloody lump.

I am grief on a sun-lit highstreet.
I don't belong.
A shade of a shade,
audaciously filling in the dappled light.

I am three days in.
For three days I have dragged this broken body
around the simpering edges
of some brave man's grave.
Oh Priam, stay your forgiveness
look what I've done to your boy.
I've left him with a body
that is a shame to bury.

Outdoor Type

You stand there   like an aborted attempt.
                    slack shouldered
An air of hesitancy hangs around the daffodils.
Mostly white, afraid to be yellow.

In this country park miasma, something about you reminds me
of the way a pumice stone reminds me
that it's a metaphor for poverty (unnecessarily overwrought).

Innumerable sorry saplings stand erect around you
like ineffectual monuments for dead soldiers.
Ill rooted substitutes,
planted by someone
tended to by someone else,
poverty stricken.
Their white bark weeps.
The sun is indifferent.
The poor bastards are begging for a eulogy.

You touch one with the palm of your shaking hand and stroke the simple wood.
You are avarice here.
Out here where the trees refuse to root.

Acknowledgements

The Boys Are Killing the Sims on the Family PC
Published as a Runner-Up in the Ledbury Poetry Prize

Lilac Bushes
Published by berlin lit

God in a Bathhouse
Published by And Other Poems

Kleptomania
Published by Magma

After a Mild Electric Shock I Think of England
Published by Strix

Recommended Reading

Anthologies

The Broken Spine Artist Collective: First Edition (2020)
The Broken Spine Artist Collective: Second Edition (2020)
The Broken Spine Artist Collective: Third Edition (2021)
The Broken Spine Artist Collective: Fourth Edition (2022)
The Broken Spine Artist Collective: Fifth Edition (2022)
BOLD: An anthology of masculinity themed creative writing (2023)
The Whiskey Tree: Untamed Nature (Wave 1) (2024)
Stage: Poetry in Response to Live Art (2024)
The Whiskey Tree: Untamed Love (Wave 1) (2024)
After House: Beat Culture Made New, (2024)

Chapbooks

Neon Ghosts (A. Parry, 2020)
The Mask (E. Horan, 2021)
Holy Things (J. Rafferty, 2022)
From This Soil (C. Bailey, 2022)
The Keeper of Aeons (M. M. C. Smith, 2022)
Four Forked Tongues (L. Aur, S. Filer, B. Lewis & E. Kemball, 2023)
Modest Raptures (E. Rees, 2023)
Surviving Death (K. Houbolt, 2023)
Twenty Seven (A. Parry, 2023)
Loggerheads (L Heuschen, 2024)

Author Biographies

Si Griffiths is a poet, writer and community organiser, from a working class background, living in Machynlleth. His poems, essays and short stories have appeared in various publications including Spelt, Lumpen and Sarai Reader. He's recently been awarded a place on Literature Wales' flagship professional development programme for under-represented writers, Representing Wales 2024-2025.

X: @ontheoutbreath
Instagram: @ontheoutbreath
linktr.ee: https://linktr.ee/sigriffiths

Wendy Sinnamon is from Portadown, Northern Ireland. She was shortlisted for the 2023 and the 2024 Seamus Heaney Award for New Writing. She has a first class BA honours in English Literature and Creative Writing. She is an ACNI recipient. Her poetry can be seen in Abridged, The Honest Ulsterman, The Waxed Lemon and Poetry Bus.

X: @iwdeatinsects
Insta: @sinnamongirl

Briony Collins is an award-winning writer and publisher. She has three books with Broken Sleep – *Blame it on Me*, *All That Glisters*, and *The Birds, The Rabbits, The Trees* – and *Whisper Network* (Bangor University) and *cactus land* (Atomic Bohemian). In 2025, her debut novel and two poetry books are forthcoming.

X: @ri_collins

Adam Panichi is based between the UK and Italy and has had work published in I'll Show You Mine, VAINE, Dust, berlin lit, Atrium, Pulp Poets Press, And Other Poems, Strix, fourteen poems and Magma. He was a runner-up in both the Ledbury and Brotherton Poetry Prizes and his debut pamphlet "Cupid, Grown" will be published by Broken Sleep Books in 2025.

X: @adam_panichi

Born, 1971, Bristol, **Matt Duggan** lives in Newport ,Wales, his poems have been included in Poetry Wales, Poetry Salzburg Review, The Poetry Review, Poetry Scotland, Stand Magazine. In 2023 Matt was shortlisted in two chapbook competitions, with a new chapbook 'The Peregrination ', due out with Dreich Publishing in Oct 2024. Matt is currently working on his fourth full length collection, for a possible 2025 release.

Jennie E. Owen's writing has been widely published online, in literary journals and anthologies. She lis a lecturer for The Open University and lives in Lancashire, UK with her husband and three children. She is a PhD student at Manchester Metropolitan University, focusing on poetry and place. *The Horses Still Run* was published by The Flight of the Dragonfly in spring, 2024.

X: @jenola101

Printed in Great Britain
by Amazon